TREE

LIFE CYCLES

Words that look like **this** can be found in the glossary on page 24.

BookLife
PUBLISHING

©2018
BookLife Publishing
King's Lynn
Norfolk PE30 4LS

All rights reserved.
Printed in Malaysia.

A catalogue record for this book is available from the British Library.

ISBN: 978-1-78637-377-9

Written by:
Holly Duhig

Edited by:
Madeline Tyler

Designed by:
Danielle Rippengill

CONTENTS

WHAT IS A LIFE CYCLE?

All animals, plants and humans go through different stages of their life as they grow and change. This is called a life cycle.

Human Life Cycle

Baby ➡ Child ➡ Adult

WHAT IS A TREE?

A tree is a type of plant that has a strong wooden trunk and branches. Many trees have leaves, flowers and fruit.

Apple Tree

SEEDS

Trees start their lives as seeds. Seeds are tree **embryos** that contain everything that is needed for a tree to grow.

Seeds need water in order to start growing.

Sycamore Seeds

Cottonwood Seeds

Seeds come from fully-grown adult trees. They come in all different shapes and sizes. Sycamore tree seeds look like little butterflies, whereas cottonwood tree seeds look fluffy.

SPROUTS

Seeds take in water until they burst. Then a root begins growing down into the soil. Roots take in **nutrients** from the soil, which help the tree to grow.

Root

After this, a stem begins to grow upwards. A very young tree is called a sprout. A sprout has a stem and a few leaves.

Much later, the stem grows into a trunk.

SAPLINGS

When a sprout has grown to one metre tall, it is called a sapling. Saplings are young trees that have started to get their woody trunk.

Sometimes saplings are tied to a post or have fences around them. This protects them from being eaten by animals or snapping in the wind.

GROWING SAPLINGS

As saplings grow, they get thicker trunks and more branches. Some saplings, like willow tree saplings, grow very fast.

Willow trees can grow up to two metres a year!

Plants make oxygen – a gas which all living things need to breathe.

Leaves use the energy they get from sunlight to make food for the plant. This, along with fresh air and water, helps them to grow.

TREES

When trees reach their full height, they are called mature trees. When trees are mature, they start producing their own seeds.

Some trees produce seeds inside an **edible** fruit. Other trees produce seeds inside hard shells. We call these nuts. Some trees make seeds in flowers or cones.

Pine Cone

Pear

Walnut

TYPES OF TREES

DECIDUOUS TREES

Some trees have leaves that turn golden-brown and fall off in the autumn. These are called deciduous trees (say: de-SID-due-us).

Deciduous trees grow new leaves in the spring.

Pine Trees

EVERGREEN TREES

Evergreen trees are trees that keep their leaves all year round. Pine trees are a type of evergreen tree. Their leaves are called needles.

TREE TRIVIA

In Hawaii there are eucalyptus trees (say: yoo-ca-lip-tus) that have rainbow-coloured **bark**.

Bonsai trees are Japanese trees that are grown to be very small. Bonsai trees are **miniature** versions of different **species** of tree.

WORLD RECORD BREAKERS

Tallest Tree

The world's tallest tree is a coast redwood tree in California called Hyperion. It is over 115 metres tall!

A Coast Redwood

Most Dangerous Tree

The record for the world's most dangerous tree belongs to the manchineel tree. The manchineel tree grows in Florida and its **sap** is **toxic**.

LIFE CYCLE OF A TREE

1 A seed takes in water until it bursts.

2 The seed grows a root and a sprout.

LIFE CYCLES

4 The sapling grows into a mature tree that can make seeds of its own.

3 The sprout grows into a sapling.

Why not try planting a tree of your own and see its life cycle for yourself? Remember to give it lots of water, sunlight and space to grow.

GLOSSARY

bark the outside cover of the trunks, branches and roots of woody plants

edible safe to be eaten

embryos unborn or unhatched young in the process of development

miniature a thing that is much smaller than normal

nutrients naturally occurring substances that are needed for plants to grow

sap a fluid that helps carry water and nutrients around a plant

species a group of very similar animals or plants that are capable of producing young together

toxic something poisonous

INDEX